plus-size garments with Style

From hoods and collars to pretty stitch patterns and lacy edgings, designer accents add chic style to fashions for curvy women. Six wardrobe favorites make up this must-have collection from Melissa Leapman.

LEISURE ARTS, INC. • Maumelle, Arkansas

tunic

EASY

SHOPPING LIST

Yarn (Medium Weight) 4 MEDIUM

[3.5 ounces, 270 yards
(100 grams, 246 meters) per skein]:

☐ {10-12}{13-14-15} skeins

Crochet Hook

☐ Size J (6 mm)
or size needed for gauge

Additional Supplies

☐ Yarn needle

SIZE INFORMATION

Sizes	Finished Chest Measurement	
Large	42"	(106.5 cm)
1X	46½"	(118 cm)
2X	49½"	(125.5 cm)
3X	54"	(137 cm)
4X	58"	(147.5 cm)

Size Note: We have printed the instructions for the sizes in different colors to make it easier for you to find:

- Size Large in Blue
- Size 1X in Pink
- Size 2X in Green
- Size 3X in Orange
- Size 4X in Brown

Instructions in Black apply to all sizes.

GAUGE INFORMATION

In pattern,
15 sts and 10 rows = 4" (10 cm)

Gauge Swatch: 4" (10 cm) square

Ch 17.

Rows 1-10: Work same as Back Body: 15 sts.

Finish off.

STITCH GUIDE

FRONT POST DOUBLE CROCHET *(abbreviated FPdc)*

YO, insert hook from **front** to **back** around post of st indicated ***(Fig. 1, page 31)***, YO and pull up a loop (3 loops on hook), (YO and draw through 2 loops on hook) twice.

BACK POST DOUBLE CROCHET *(abbreviated BPdc)*

YO, insert hook from **back** to **front** around post of st indicated ***(Fig. 1, page 31)***, YO and pull up a loop (3 loops on hook), (YO and draw through 2 loops on hook) twice.

HALF DOUBLE CROCHET 2 TOGETHER *(abbreviated hdc2tog)* (uses next 2 sts)

(YO, insert hook in **next** st, YO and pull up a loop) twice, YO and draw through all 5 loops on hook **(counts as one hdc)**.

BACK

BODY

Ch {81-89}{95-103-111}.

Row 1 (Right side)**:** Dc in fourth ch from hook **(3 skipped chs count as first dc)** and in each ch across: {79-87}{93-101-109} dc.

Note: Loop a short piece of yarn around any stitch to mark Row 1 as **right** side.

Row 2: Ch 2 **(counts as first hdc, now and throughout)**, turn; work FPdc around next st, (work BPdc around next st, work FPdc around next st) across to last st, hdc in last st.

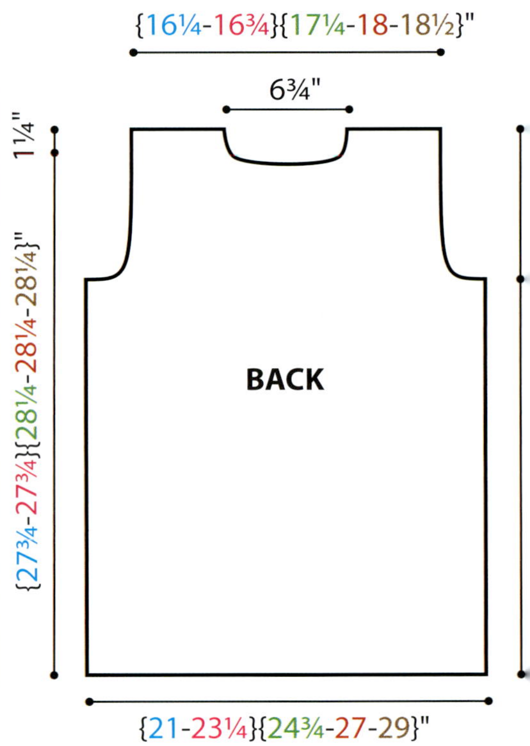

Repeat Row 2 for pattern until Body measures approximately {21-20½}{20½-20-19½}"/{53.5-52}{52-51-49.5} cm from beginning ch, ending by working a **wrong** side row.

ARMHOLE SHAPING

Maintain established pattern throughout.

Row 1: Turn; slip st in first {4-5}{6-7-8} sts, ch 2, work across to last {4-5}{6-7-8} sts, hdc in next st, leave remaining sts unworked: {73-79}{83-89-95} sts.

Row 2: Turn; slip st in first {3-4}{5-6-7} sts, ch 2, work across to last {3-4}{5-6-7} sts, hdc in next st, leave remaining sts unworked: {69-73}{75-79-83} sts.

Row 3 (Decrease row)**:** Ch 2, turn; hdc2tog, work across to last 3 sts, hdc2tog, hdc in last hdc: {67-71}{73-77-81} sts.

Repeat Row 3, {1-2}{2-3-6} time(s): {65-67}{69-71-69} sts.

SIZES LARGE, 1X, 2X, & 3X ONLY

Continue to decrease one stitch at **each** edge in same manner, every other row twice: {61-63}{65-67} sts.

ALL SIZES

Work even until Back measures approximately {27¾-27¾} {28¼-28¼-28¼}"/{70.5-70.5} {72-72-72} cm from beginning ch, ending by working a **wrong** side row.

RIGHT NECK SHAPING

Row 1: Ch 2, turn; work across next {17-18}{19-20-21} sts, hdc in next st, leave remaining sts unworked: {19-20}{21-22-23} sts.

Row 2: Ch 2, turn; hdc2tog, work across to last hdc, hdc in last hdc: {18-19}{20-21-22} sts.

Row 3: Ch 2, turn; work across to last hdc, hdc in last hdc; finish off.

LEFT NECK SHAPING

Row 1: With **right** side facing, skip 23 sts from Right Neck Shaping and join yarn with slip st in next st; ch 2, work across to last hdc, hdc in last hdc: {19-20}{21-22-23} sts.

Row 2: Ch 2, turn; work across to last 3 sts, hdc2tog, hdc in last hdc: {18-19} {20-21-22} sts.

Row 3: Ch 2, turn; work across to last hdc, hdc in last hdc; finish off.

FRONT

Work same as Back through Row 3 of Armhole Shaping: {67-71}{73-77-81} sts.

SIZE LARGE ONLY

RIGHT NECK SHAPING

Row 1: Ch 2, turn; hdc2tog, work across next 24 sts, hdc in next st, leave remaining sts unworked: 27 sts.

Row 2: Turn; slip st in first 4 sts, ch 2, work across to last hdc, hdc in last hdc: 24 sts.

Row 3: Ch 2, turn; hdc2tog, work across to last 3 sts, hdc in next st, leave last 2 sts unworked: 21 sts.

Row 4: Ch 2, turn; work across to last hdc, hdc in last hdc.

Row 5: Ch 2, turn; hdc2tog, work across to last 3 sts, hdc2tog, hdc in last hdc: 19 sts.

Row 6: Ch 2, turn; work across to last hdc, hdc in last hdc.

Row 7: Ch 2, turn; work across to last 3 sts, hdc2tog, hdc in last hdc: 18 sts.

Work even until Armhole measures same as Back, ending by working a **right** side row; finish off leaving a long end for sewing.

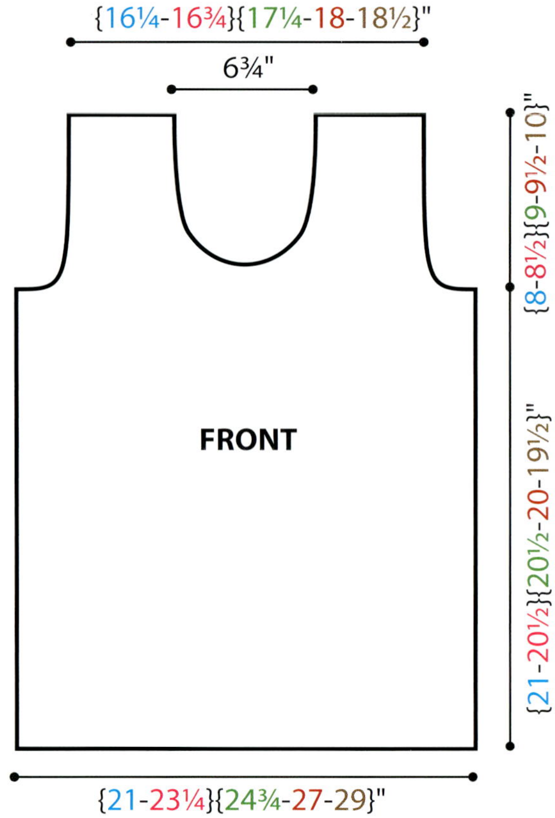

LEFT NECK SHAPING

Row 1: With **wrong** side facing, skip 11 sts from Right Neck Shaping and join yarn with slip st in next st; ch 2, work across to last 3 sts, hdc2tog, hdc in last hdc: 27 sts.

Row 2: Ch 2, turn; work across to last 4 sts, hdc in next st, leave last 3 sts unworked: 24 sts.

Row 3: Turn; slip st in first 3 sts, ch 2, work across to last 3 sts, hdc2tog, hdc in last hdc: 21 sts.

Row 4: Ch 2, turn; work across to last hdc, hdc in last hdc.

Row 5: Ch 2, turn; hdc2tog, work across to last 3 sts, hdc2tog, hdc in last hdc: 19 sts.

Row 6: Ch 2, turn; work across to last hdc, hdc in last hdc.

Row 7: Ch 2, turn; hdc2tog, work across to last hdc, hdc in last hdc: 18 sts.

Work even until Left Neck Shaping measures same as Right Neck Shaping, ending by working a **right** side row; finish off leaving a long end for sewing.

SIZES 1X & 2X ONLY

Rows 4 and 5: Repeat Row 3 twice: {67}{69} sts.

RIGHT NECK SHAPING

Row 1: Ch 2, turn; hdc in next {26}{27} sts, hdc in next st, leave remaining sts unworked: {28}{29} sts.

Row 2: Turn; slip st in first 4 sts, ch 2, work across to last 3 sts, hdc2tog, hdc in last hdc: {24}{25} sts.

Row 3: Ch 2, turn; work across to last 3 sts, hdc in next st, leave last 2 sts unworked: {22}{23} sts.

Rows 4 and 5: Ch 2, turn; work across to last 3 sts, hdc2tog, hdc in last hdc: {20}{21} sts.

Row 6: Ch 2, turn; work across to last hdc, hdc in last hdc.

Row 7: Ch 2, turn; work across to last 3 sts, hdc2tog, hdc in last hdc: {19}{20} sts.

Work even until Armhole measures same as Back, ending by working a **right** side row; finish off leaving a long end for sewing.

LEFT NECK SHAPING

Row 1: With **wrong** side facing, skip 11 sts from Right Neck Shaping and join yarn with slip st in next st; ch 2, work across to last hdc, hdc in last hdc: {28}{29} sts.

Row 2: Ch 2, turn; hdc2tog, work across to last 4 sts, hdc in next st, leave last 3 sts unworked: {24}{25} sts.

Row 3: Turn; slip st in first 3 sts, ch 2, work across to last hdc, hdc in last hdc: {22}{23} sts.

Rows 4 and 5: Ch 2, turn; hdc2tog, work across to last hdc, hdc in last hdc: {20}{21} sts.

Row 6: Ch 2, turn; work across to last hdc, hdc in last hdc.

Row 7: Ch 2, turn; hdc2tog, work across to last hdc, hdc in last hdc: {19}{20} sts.

Work even until Left Neck Shaping measures same as Right Neck Shaping, ending by working a **wrong** side row; finish off leaving a long end for sewing.

SIZE 3X ONLY

Rows 4-6: Repeat Row 3, 3 times: 71 sts.

Row 7: Ch 2, turn; work across to last hdc, hdc in last hdc.

RIGHT NECK SHAPING

Row 1: Ch 2, turn; hdc2tog, hdc in next 26 sts, hdc in next st, leave remaining sts unworked: 29 sts.

Row 2: Turn; slip st in first 4 sts, ch 2, work across to last hdc, hdc in last hdc: 26 sts.

Row 3: Ch 2, turn; hdc2tog, work across to last 3 sts, hdc in next st, leave last 2 sts unworked: 23 sts.

Row 4: Ch 2, turn; work across to last hdc, hdc in last hdc.

Row 5 (Decrease row)**:** Ch 2, turn; work across to last 3 sts, hdc2tog, hdc in last hdc: 22 sts.

Rows 6 and 7: Repeat Rows 4 and 5: 21 sts.

Work even until Armhole measures same as Back, ending by working a **right** side row; finish off leaving a long end for sewing.

LEFT NECK SHAPING

Row 1: With **wrong** side facing, skip 11 sts from Right Neck Shaping and join yarn with slip st in next st; ch 2, work across to last 3 sts, hdc2tog, hdc in last hdc: 29 sts.

Row 2: Ch 2, turn; work across to last 4 sts, hdc in next st, leave last 3 sts unworked: 26 sts.

Row 3: Turn; slip st in first 3 sts, ch 2, work across to last 3 sts, hdc2tog, hdc in last hdc: 23 sts.

Row 4: Ch 2, turn; work across to last hdc, hdc in last hdc.

Row 5 (Decrease row)**:** Ch 2, turn; hdc2tog, work across to last hdc, hdc in last hdc: 22 sts.

Rows 6 and 7: Repeat Rows 4 and 5: 21 sts.

Work even until Left Neck Shaping measures same as Right Neck Shaping, ending by working a **right** side row; finish off leaving a long end for sewing.

SIZE 4X ONLY

Rows 4-7: Repeat Row 3, 4 times: 73 sts.

RIGHT NECK SHAPING

Row 1: Ch 2, turn; hdc2tog, work across next 27 sts, hdc in next st, leave remaining sts unworked: 30 sts.

Row 2: Turn; slip st in first 4 sts, ch 2, work across to last 3 sts, hdc2tog, hdc in last hdc: 26 sts.

Row 3: Ch 2, turn; work across to last 3 sts, hdc in next st, leave last 2 sts unworked: 24 sts.

Row 4: Ch 2, turn; work across to last hdc, hdc in last hdc.

Row 5 (Decrease row)**:** Ch 2, turn; work across to last 3 sts, hdc2tog, hdc in last hdc: 23 sts.

Rows 6 and 7: Repeat Rows 4 and 5: 22 sts.

Work even until Armhole measures same as Back, ending by working a **right** side row; finish off leaving a long end for sewing.

LEFT NECK SHAPING

Row 1: With **wrong** side facing, skip 11 sts from Right Neck Shaping and join yarn with slip st in next st; ch 2, work across to last 3 sts, hdc2tog, hdc in last hdc: 30 sts.

Row 2: Ch 2, turn; hdc2tog, work across to last 4 sts, hdc in next st, leave last 3 sts unworked: 26 sts.

Row 3: Turn; slip st in first 3 sts, ch 2, work across to last hdc, hdc in last hdc: 24 sts.

Row 4: Ch 2, turn; work across to last hdc, hdc in last hdc.

Row 5 (Decrease row)**:** Ch 2, turn; hdc2tog, work across to last hdc, hdc in last hdc: 23 sts.

Rows 6 and 7: Repeat Rows 4 and 5: 22 sts.

Work even until Left Neck Shaping measures same as Right Neck Shaping, ending by working a **right** side row; finish off leaving a long end for sewing.

SLEEVE (Make 2)

BODY

Ch {37-39}{39-39-39}.

Row 1 (Right side)**:** Dc in fourth ch from hook **(3 skipped chs count as first dc)** and in each ch across: {35-37}{37-37-37} dc.

Note: Mark Row 1 as **right** side.

Row 2: Ch 2, turn; work FPdc around next st, (work BPdc around next st, work FPdc around next st) across to last st, hdc in last st.

Row 3 (Increase row)**:** Ch 2, turn; hdc in first hdc, work FPdc around next st, (work BPdc around next st, work FPdc around next st) across to last hdc, 2 hdc in last hdc: {37-39}{39-39-39} sts.

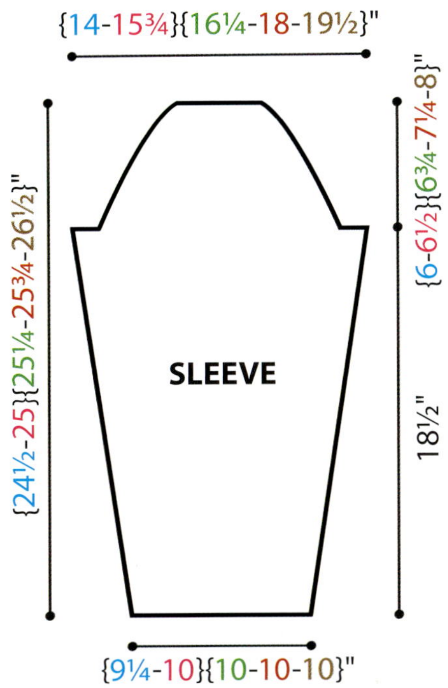

Row 4: Ch 2, turn; work BPdc around next st, (work FPdc around next st, work BPdc around next st) across to last hdc, hdc in last hdc.

Working in established pattern, continue to increase one stitch at **each** edge, every other row, {0-0}{2-8-14} times ***(see Zeros, page 30)***; then increase every fourth row, {4-10}{9-6-3} times; then increase every sixth row, {4-0}{0-0-0} times: {53-59}{61-67-73} sts.

Work even until Body measures approximately 18½" (47 cm) from beginning ch, ending by working a **wrong** side row.

SLEEVE CAP

Maintain established pattern throughout.

Row 1: Turn; slip st in first {5-6}{7-8-9} sts, ch 2, work across to last {5-6}{7-8-9} sts, hdc in next st, leave remaining sts unworked: {45-49}{49-53-57} sts.

Row 2 (Decrease row)**:** Ch 2, turn; hdc2tog twice, work across to last 5 sts, hdc2tog twice, hdc in last hdc: {41-45}{45-49-53} sts.

Continue to decrease **two** stitches at **each** edge in same manner, every row, {0-1}{0-1-1} time(s); then decrease **one** stitch, every row, {11-11}{13-13-15} times: 19 sts.

Last 2 Rows: Turn; slip st in first 3 sts, ch 2, work across to last 3 sts, hdc in next st, leave last 2 sts unworked: 11 sts.

Finish off.

FINISHING

Whipstitch Front to Back at shoulders ***(Fig. 3a, page 31)***.

NECK EDGING

Rnd 1: With **right** side facing, join yarn with slip st at left shoulder seam; ch 1, sc evenly around; join with slip st to first sc.

Rnd 2: Ch 1, do **not** turn; working from **left** to **right**, work reverse sc in each sc around ***(Figs. 4a-d, page 31)***; join with slip st to first st, finish off.

Sew Sleeves to Armholes, matching center of last row on Sleeve Cap to shoulder seam.

Beginning at Sleeve edge, whipstitch underarm and side in one continuous seam ***(Fig. 3b, page 31)***, leaving last 5" (12.5 cm) open.

unconstructed jacket

EASY

SHOPPING LIST

Yarn (Super Fine Weight) SUPER FINE 1

[3.5 ounces, 438 yards (100 grams, 400 meters) per skein]:

- ☐ {6-7}{7-8-9} skeins

Crochet Hook

- ☐ Size D (3.25 mm) **or** size needed for gauge

Additional Supplies

- ☐ Tapestry needle

SIZE INFORMATION

Sizes	Finished Chest Measurement	
Large	42"	(106.5 cm)
1X	45¾"	(116 cm)
2X	50¼"	(127.5 cm)
3X	54"	(137 cm)
4X	58"	(147.5 cm)

Size Note: We have printed the instructions for the sizes in different colors to make it easier for you to find:

- Size Large in Blue
- Size 1X in Pink
- Size 2X in Green
- Size 3X in Orange
- Size 4X in Brown

Instructions in Black apply to all sizes.

GAUGE INFORMATION

In pattern,
21 sts and 22 rows = 4" (10 cm)

Gauge Swatch: 4¼"w x 4"h (10.75 cm x 10 cm)

Ch 23.

Rows 1-22: Work same as Back Body: 22 sts.

Finish off.

STITCH GUIDE

HALF DOUBLE CROCHET 2 TOGETHER ***(abbreviated hdc2tog)*** (uses next 2 sts)

(YO, insert hook in **next** st, YO and pull up a loop) twice, YO and draw through all 5 loops on hook **(counts as one hdc)**.

BACK

BODY

Ch {111-121}{133-143-153}.

Row 1 (Right side)**:** Sc in third ch from hook **(2 skipped chs count as first hdc)**, dc in next ch, (sc in next ch, dc in next ch) across to last ch, hdc in last ch: {110-120}{132-142-152} sts.

Note: Loop a short piece of yarn around any stitch to mark Row 1 as **right** side.

Row 2: Ch 2 **(counts as first hdc, now and throughout)**, turn; (sc in next dc, dc in next sc) across to last hdc, hdc in last hdc.

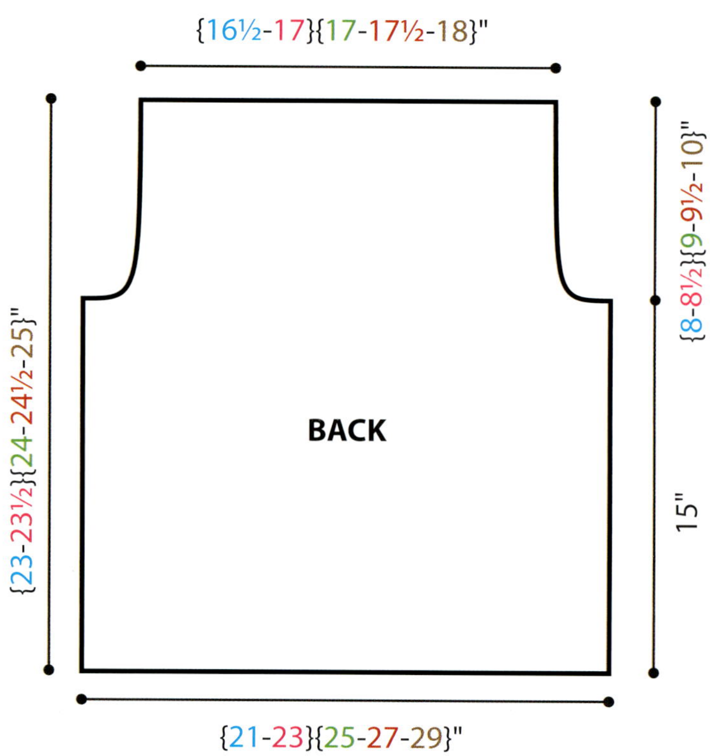

Repeat Row 2 for pattern until Body measures approximately 15" (38 cm) from beginning ch, ending by working a **wrong** side row.

ARMHOLE SHAPING

Maintain established pattern throughout.

Row 1: Turn; slip st in first {6-7}{8-9-10} sts, ch 2, work across to last {6-7}{8-9-10} sts, hdc in next st, leave remaining sts unworked: {100-108}{118-126-134} sts.

Row 2: Turn; slip st in first {4-5}{6-6-8} sts, ch 2, work across to last {4-5}{6-6-8} sts, hdc in next st, leave remaining sts unworked: {94-100}{108-116-120} sts.

Row 3 (Decrease row)**:** Ch 2, turn; hdc2tog, work across to last 3 sts, hdc2tog, hdc in last st: {92-98}{106-114-118} sts.

Repeat Row 3, {0-0}{5-8-9} times ***(see Zeros, page 30)***: {96-98-100} sts.

Continue to decrease one stitch at **each** edge in same manner, every other row, {3-4}{3-3-3} times: {86-90}{90-92-94} sts.

Work even until Back measures approximately {23-23½}{24-24½-25}"/{58.5-59.5}{61-62-63.5} cm from beginning ch, ending by working a **wrong** side row; finish off leaving a long end for sewing.

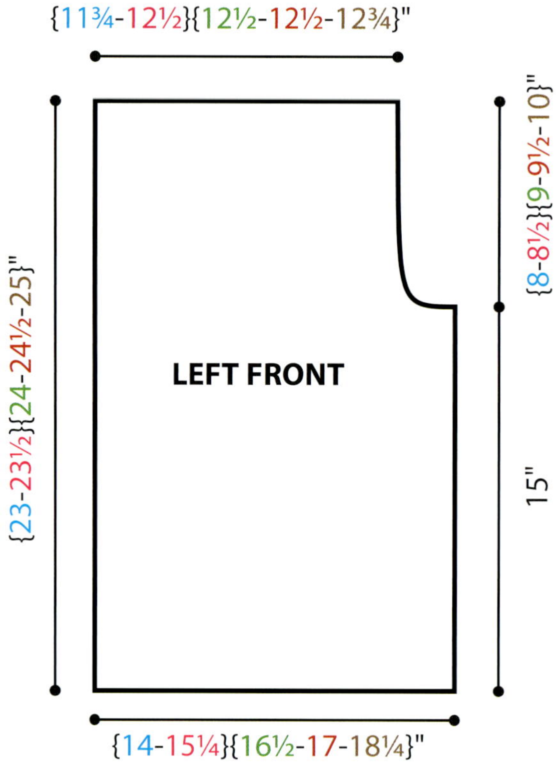

LEFT FRONT
BODY

Ch {75-81}{87-91-97}.

Work same as Back to Armhole Shaping: {74-80}{86-90-96} sts.

ARMHOLE SHAPING

Maintain established pattern throughout.

Row 1: Turn; slip st in first {6-7}{8-9-10} sts, ch 2, work across to last hdc, hdc in last hdc: {69-74}{79-82-87} sts.

Row 2: Ch 2, turn; work across to last {4-5}{6-6-8} sts, hdc in next st, leave remaining sts unworked: {66-70}{74-77-80} sts.

Row 3 (Decrease row)**:** Ch 2, turn; hdc2tog, work across to last hdc, hdc in last hdc: {65-69}{73-76-79} sts.

Continue to decrease one stitch at Armhole edge in same manner, every row, {0-0}{5-8-9} times; then decrease, every other row, {3-4}{3-3-3} times: {62-65}{65-65-67} sts.

Work even until Left Front measures same as Back, ending by working a **wrong** side row; finish off leaving a long end for sewing.

RIGHT FRONT
BODY

Ch {75-81}{87-91-97}.

Work same as Back to Armhole Shaping: {74-80}{86-90-96} sts.

ARMHOLE SHAPING

Maintain established pattern throughout.

Row 1: Ch 2, turn; work across to last {6-7}{8-9-10} sts, hdc in next st, leave remaining sts unworked: {69-74}{79-82-87} sts.

Row 2: Turn; slip st in first {4-5}{6-6-8} sts, ch 2, work across to last hdc, hdc in last hdc: {66-70}{74-77-80} sts.

Row 3 (Decrease row)**:** Ch 2, turn; work across to last 3 sts, hdc2tog, hdc in last hdc: {65-69}{73-76-79} sts.

Continue to decrease one stitch at Armhole edge in same manner, every row, {0-0}{5-8-9} times; then decrease, every other row, {3-4}{3-3-3} times: {62-65}{65-65-67} sts.

Work even until Right Front measures same as Back, ending by working a **wrong** side row; finish off.

SLEEVE (Make 2)

BODY

Ch {51-53}{53-53-57}.

Row 1 (Right side)**:** Sc in third ch from hook **(2 skipped chs count as first hdc)**, dc in next ch, (sc in next ch, dc in next ch) across to last ch, hdc in last ch: {50-52}{52-52-56} sts.

Note: Mark Row 1 as **right** side.

Row 2: Ch 2, turn; (sc in next dc, dc in next sc) across to last hdc, hdc in last hdc.

Repeat Row 2, {5-3}{1-1-1} time(s).

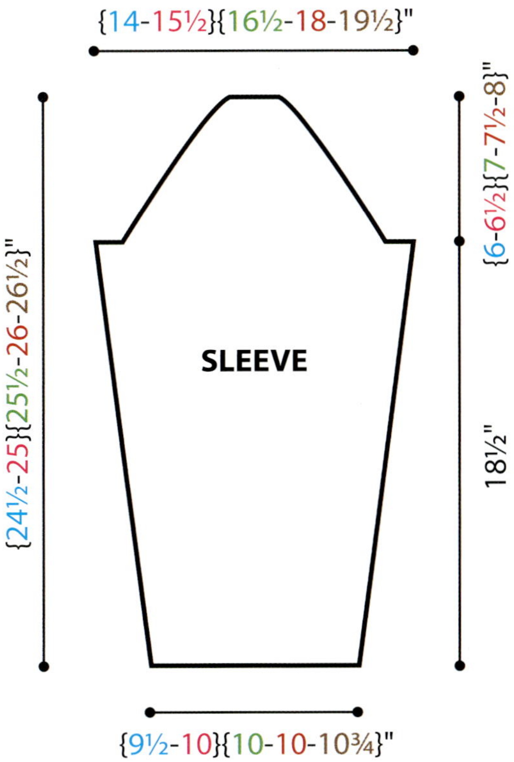

Maintain established pattern throughout.

Increase Row: Ch 2, turn; hdc in first hdc, work across to last hdc, 2 hdc in last hdc: {52-54}{54-54-58} sts.

Continue to increase one stitch at **each** edge in same manner, every fourth row, {0-0}{2-14-20} times; then increase every sixth row, {0-11}{14-6-2} times; then increase every eighth row, {11-3}{0-0-0} times: {74-82}{86-94-102} sts.

Work even until Body measures approximately 18½" (47 cm) from beginning ch, ending by working a **wrong** side row.

SLEEVE CAP

Row 1: Turn; slip st in first {6-7}{8-9-10} sts, ch 2, work across to last {6-7}{8-9-10} sts, hdc in next st, leave remaining sts unworked: {64-70}{72-78-84} sts.

Row 2 (Decrease row)**:** Ch 2, turn; hdc2tog, work across to last 3 sts, hdc2tog, hdc in last hdc: {62-68}{70-76-82} sts.

Repeat Row 2, {5-8}{8-11-14} times: {52-52}{54-54-54} sts.

Continue to decrease one stitch at **each** edge in same manner, every other row, {12-12}{13-13-13} times: 28 sts.

Last 2 Rows: Turn; slip st in first 4 sts, ch 2, work across to last 4 sts, hdc in next st, leave remaining sts unworked: 16 sts.

Finish off.

FINISHING

Whipstitch Front to Back at shoulders, working across {26-28}{28-29-30} sts ***(Fig. 3a, page 31)***.

Sew Sleeves to Armholes, matching center of last row on Sleeve Cap to shoulder seam.

Whipstitch underarm and side in one continuous seam ***(Fig. 3b, page 31)***.

Top Front corners can be folded to form a lapel and tacked in place.

boxy cardi

EASY

SHOPPING LIST

Yarn (Medium Weight) MEDIUM 4

[3 ounces, 149 yards (85 grams, 136 meters) per skein]:

☐ {8-9}{11-12-13} skeins

Crochet Hook

☐ Size I (5.5 mm) **or** size needed for gauge

Additional Supplies

☐ Yarn needle

☐ Sewing needle and thread

☐ 1¼" (32 mm) Buttons - 3

SIZE INFORMATION

Sizes	Finished Chest Measurement	
Large	42"	(106.5 cm)
1X	46"	(117 cm)
2X	50"	(127 cm)
3X	54"	(137 cm)
4X	58"	(147.5 cm)

Size Note: We have printed the instructions for the sizes in different colors to make it easier for you to find:

- Size Large in Blue
- Size 1X in Pink
- Size 2X in Green
- Size 3X in Orange
- Size 4X in Brown

Instructions in Black apply to all sizes.

GAUGE INFORMATION

12 hdc and 8 rows = 4" (10 cm)

Gauge Swatch: 4" (10 cm) square

Ch 13.

Row 1: Hdc in third ch from hook **(2 skipped chs count as first hdc)** and in each ch across: 12 hdc.

Rows 2-8: Ch 2 **(counts as first hdc)**, turn; hdc in next hdc and in each hdc across.

Finish off.

STITCH GUIDE

FRONT POST TREBLE CROCHET ***(abbreviated FPtr)***

YO twice, insert hook from **front** to **back** around post of st indicated ***(Fig. 1, page 31)***, YO and pull up a loop (4 loops on hook), (YO and draw through 2 loops on hook) 3 times.

FRONT POST DOUBLE TREBLE CROCHET ***(abbreviated FPdtr)***

YO 3 times, insert hook from **front** to **back** around post of st indicated ***(Fig. 1, page 31)***, YO and pull up a loop (5 loops on hook), (YO and draw through 2 loops on hook) 4 times.

HALF DOUBLE CROCHET 2 TOGETHER ***(abbreviated hdc2tog)***

(uses next 2 sts)

(YO, insert hook in **next** st, YO and pull up a loop) twice, YO and draw through all 5 loops on hook **(counts as one hdc)**.

BACK

BODY

Ch {64-70}{76-82-88}.

Row 1 (Right side)**:** Hdc in third ch from hook **(2 skipped chs count as first hdc, now and throughout)** and in each ch across: {63-69}{75-81-87} hdc.

Note: Loop a short piece of yarn around any stitch to mark Row 1 as **right** side.

Row 2: Ch 2 **(counts as first hdc, now and throughout)**, turn; hdc in next hdc and in each hdc across.

Repeat Row 2 until Body measures approximately 14" (35.5 cm) from beginning ch, ending by working a **wrong** side row.

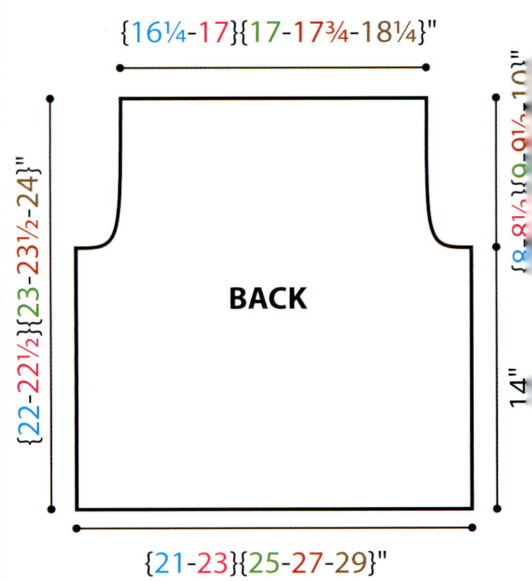

ARMHOLE SHAPING

Row 1: Turn; slip st in first {4-5}{6-7-8} hdc, ch 2, hdc in next hdc and in each hdc across to last {3-4}{5-6-7} hdc, leave remaining hdc unworked: {57-61}{65-69-73} hdc.

Row 2: Turn; slip st in first {3-3}{4-4-5} hdc, ch 2, hdc in next hdc and in each hdc across to last {2-2}{3-3-4} hdc, leave remaining hdc unworked: {53-57}{59-63-65} hdc.

Row 3 (Decrease row)**:** Ch 2, turn; hdc2tog, hdc in each hdc across to last 3 hdc, hdc2tog, hdc in last hdc: {51-55}{57-61-63} hdc.

Repeat Row 3, {0-1}{2-4-4} times ***(see Zeros, page 30)***: {53}{53-53-55} hdc.

SIZES LARGE, 1X, & 2X ONLY

Next Row: Ch 2, turn; hdc in next hdc and in each hdc across.

Next Row: Repeat Row 3: {49-51}{51} hdc.

ALL SIZES

Work even until Back measures approximately {22-22½}{23-23½-24}"/{56-57}{58.5-59.5-61} cm from beginning ch, ending by working a **wrong** side row; finish off.

LEFT FRONT

BODY

Ch {37-39}{43-45-49}.

Row 1 (Right side)**:** Hdc in third ch from hook and in each ch across: {36-38}{42-44-48} hdc.

Note: Mark Row 1 as **right** side.

Row 2: Ch 2, turn; hdc in next hdc and in each hdc across.

Row 3: Ch 2, turn; hdc in next {11-14}{17-19-22} hdc, work FPtr around each of 4 hdc on row **below** next 4 hdc (Row 1), skip 4 hdc behind FPtr, hdc in next hdc and in each hdc across.

Row 4: Ch 2, turn; hdc in next hdc and in each st across.

Row 5: Ch 2, turn; hdc in next {9-12}{15-17-20} hdc, work FPdtr around each of next 2 FPtr 2 rows **below**, skip 2 hdc behind FPdtr, hdc in next 4 hdc, work FPdtr around each of next 2 FPtr 2 rows **below**, skip 2 hdc behind FPdtr, hdc in next hdc and in each hdc across.

Row 6: Ch 2, turn; hdc in next hdc and in each st across.

Row 7: Ch 2, turn; hdc in next {7-10}{13-15-18} hdc, work FPdtr around each of next 2 FPdtr 2 rows **below**, skip 2 hdc behind FPdtr, hdc in next

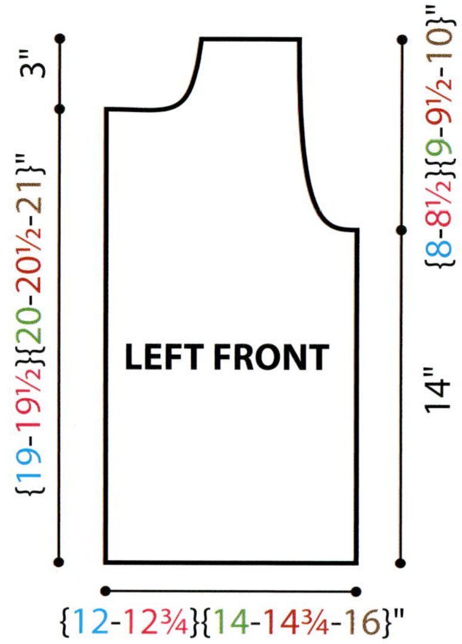

2 hdc, work FPtr around each of 4 hdc on row **below** next 4 hdc, skip 4 hdc behind FPtr, hdc in next 2 hdc, work FPdtr around each of next 2 FPdtr 2 rows **below**, skip 2 hdc behind FPdtr, hdc in next hdc and in each hdc across.

Repeat Rows 4-7 for pattern until Left Front measures same as Back to Armhole Shaping, ending by working a **wrong** side row.

ARMHOLE SHAPING

Maintain established pattern throughout.

Row 1: Turn; slip st in first {4-5}{6-7-8} hdc, ch 2, work across: {33-34}{37-38-41} sts.

Row 2: Ch 2, turn; hdc in next hdc and in each st across to last {2-2}{3-3-4} hdc, leave remaining hdc unworked: {31-32}{34-35-37} hdc.

Row 3 (Decrease row)**:** Ch 2, turn; hdc2tog, work across: {30-31}{33-34-36} sts.

Continue to decrease one stitch at Armhole edge, every row, {0-1}{2-4-4} time(s); then decrease, every other row, {1-1}{1-0-0} time(s): {29-29}{30-30-32} sts.

Work even until Left Front measures approximately {19-19½}{20-20½-21}"/{48.5-49.5}{51-52-53.5} cm from beginning ch, ending by working a **wrong** side row.

NECK SHAPING

Row 1: Ch 2, turn; work across to last {8-7}{8-7-8} hdc, leave remaining hdc unworked: {21-22}{22-23-24} sts.

Row 2: Turn; slip st in first 4 hdc, ch 2, hdc in next hdc and in each st across: {18-19}{19-20-21} hdc.

Row 3: Ch 2, turn; work across to last 3 hdc, hdc2tog, hdc in last hdc: {17-18}{18-19-20} sts.

Row 4: Ch 2, turn; hdc2tog, hdc in each st across: {16-17}{17-18-19} hdc.

Row 5: Ch 2, turn; work across.

Row 6: Ch 2, turn; hdc in next hdc and in each st across; finish off leaving a long end for sewing.

Place markers for 3 buttons, placing one 10½" (26.5 cm) from the bottom edge, one on the third to the last row before the Neck Shaping, and one centered between both markers.

RIGHT FRONT

BODY

Ch {37-39}{43-45-49}.

Row 1 (Right side)**:** Hdc in third ch from hook and in each ch across: {36-38}{42-44-48} hdc.

Note: Mark Row 1 as **right** side.

Row 2: Ch 2, turn; hdc in next hdc and in each hdc across.

Row 3: Ch 2, turn; hdc in next {19-18}{19-19-20} hdc, work FPtr around each of 4 hdc on row **below** next 4 hdc (Row 1), skip 4 hdc behind FPtr, hdc in next hdc and in each hdc across.

Row 4: Ch 2, turn; hdc in next hdc and in each st across.

Row 5: Ch 2, turn; hdc in next {17-16}{17-17-18} hdc, work FPdtr around each of next 2 FPtr 2 rows **below**, skip 2 hdc behind FPdtr, hdc in next 4 hdc, work FPdtr around each of next 2 FPtr 2 rows **below**, skip 2 hdc behind FPdtr, hdc in next hdc and in each hdc across.

Row 6: Ch 2, turn; hdc in next hdc and in each st across.

Row 7: Ch 2, turn; hdc in next {15-14}{15-15-16} hdc, work FPdtr around each of next 2 FPdtr 2 rows **below**, skip 2 hdc behind FPdtr, hdc in next 2 hdc, work FPtr around each of 4 hdc on row **below** next 4 hdc, skip 4 hdc behind FPtr, hdc in next 2 hdc, work FPdtr around each of next 2 FPdtr 2 rows **below**, skip 2 hdc behind FPdtr, hdc in next hdc and in each hdc across.

Repeat Rows 4-7 for pattern until Right Front measures approximately 10½" (26.5 cm) from beginning ch, ending by working a **right** side row.

Buttonhole Row: Ch 2, turn; hdc in next hdc and in each st across to last 4 hdc, ch 2, skip next 2 hdc **(buttonhole made)**, hdc in last 2 hdc: {34-36}{40-42-46} hdc and one ch-2 sp.

Next Row: Ch 2, turn; hdc in next hdc, 2 hdc in next ch-2 sp, work across: {36-38}{42-44-48} sts.

Work two more buttonholes when Right Front measures same as markers on Left Front.

Work even until Right Front measures same as Left Front to Armhole Shaping, ending by working a **wrong** side row.

ARMHOLE SHAPING

Maintain established pattern throughout.

Row 1: Ch 2, turn; work across to last {3-4}{5-6-7} hdc, leave remaining hdc unworked: {33-34}{37-38-41} sts.

Row 2: Turn; slip st in first {3-3}{4-4-5} hdc, ch 2, hdc in next hdc and in each st across: {31-32}{34-35-37} hdc.

Row 3 (Decrease row)**:** Ch 2, turn; work across to last 3 hdc, hdc2tog, hdc in last hdc: {30-31}{33-34-36} sts.

Continue to decrease one stitch at Armhole edge, every row, {0-1}{2-4-4} time(s); then decrease, every other row, {1-1}{1-0-0} times: {29-29}{30-30-32} sts.

Work even until Right Front measures same as Left Front to Neck Shaping, ending by working a **wrong** side row.

NECK SHAPING

Row 1: Turn; slip st in first {9-8} {9-8-9} hdc, ch 2, work across: {21-22} {22-23-24} sts.

Row 2: Ch 2, turn; hdc in next hdc and in each st across to last 3 hdc, leave last 3 hdc unworked: {18-19} {19-20-21} hdc.

Row 3: Ch 2, turn; hdc2tog, work across: {17-18}{18-19-20} sts.

Row 4: Ch 2, turn; hdc in next hdc and in each st across to last 3 hdc, hdc2tog, hdc in last hdc: {16-17} {17-18-19} hdc.

Row 5: Ch 2, turn; work across.

Row 6: Ch 2, turn; hdc in next hdc and in each st across; finish off leaving a long end for sewing.

SLEEVE (Make 2)

BODY

Ch {43-47}{51-55-59}.

Row 1 (Right side)**:** Hdc in third ch from hook and in each ch across: {42-46}{50-54-58} hdc.

Note: Mark Row 1 as **right** side.

Row 2: Ch 2, turn; hdc in next hdc and in each hdc across.

Repeat Row 2 until Body measures approximately 14" (35.5 cm) from beginning ch, ending by working a **wrong** side row.

SLEEVE CAP

Row 1: Turn; slip st in first {4-5} {6-7-8} hdc, ch 2, hdc in next hdc and in each hdc across to last {3-4} {5-6-7} hdc, leave remaining hdc unworked: {36-38}{40-42-44} hdc.

Row 2 (Decrease row)**:** Ch 2, turn; hdc2tog, hdc across to last 3 hdc, hdc2tog, hdc in last hdc: {34-36} {38-40-42} hdc.

Repeat Row 2, {8-9}{10-11-12} times: 18 sts.

Last 2 Rows: Turn; slip st in first 3 sts, ch 2, hdc in next hdc and in each hdc across to last 2 hdc, leave last 2 hdc unworked: 10 hdc.

Finish off.

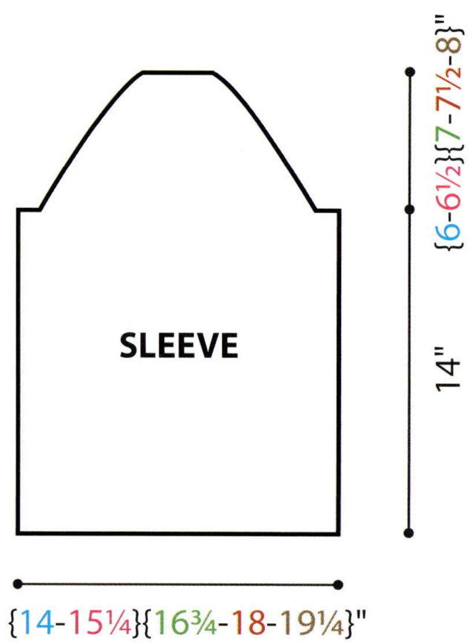

FINISHING

If a smooth yarn was not used for this garment, one of matching color can be used for all seams.

Whipstitch Front to Back at shoulders *(Fig. 3a, page 31)*.

COLLAR

Row 1: With **wrong** side facing, join yarn with slip st in first unworked hdc on Left Front Neck Shaping; ch 2, hdc evenly around to same point on Right Front Neck Shaping.

Row 2 (Increase row)**:** Ch 2, turn; hdc in first st and in each hdc across to last hdc, 2 hdc in last hdc.

Continue to increase one stitch at **each** edge, every third row, 3 times; then increase every other row twice.

Finish off.

Sew Sleeves to Armholes, matching center of last row on Sleeve Cap to shoulder seam.

Whipstitch underarm and side in one continuous seam *(Fig. 3b, page 31)*.

Sew buttons to Left Front at markers.

drapey vest

EASY

SHOPPING LIST

Yarn (Light Weight) LIGHT 3

[3.5 ounces, 254 yards (100 grams, 232 meters) per skein]:

- ☐ {6-7}{7-8-9} skeins

Crochet Hooks

- ☐ Size G (4 mm)
- ☐ Size H (5 mm)

or sizes needed for gauge

SIZE INFORMATION

The Fronts are extra wide to create the drape. The Back measurement is given from center of one armhole to the center of the other armhole.

Sizes	Finished Back Measurement
Large	17¾" (45 cm)
1X	18¼" (46.5 cm)
2X	18¾" (47.5 cm)
3X	19¼" (49 cm)
4X	19¾" (50 cm)

Size Note: We have printed the instructions for the sizes in different colors to make it easier for you to find:

- Size Large in Blue
- Size 1X in Pink
- Size 2X in Green
- Size 3X in Orange
- Size 4X in Brown

Instructions in Black apply to all sizes.

GAUGE INFORMATION

With larger size hook,
14 hdc and 10 rows = 4" (10 cm)

Gauge Swatch: 4" (10 cm) square
With larger size hook, ch 15.
Row 1: Hdc in third ch from hook **(2 skipped chs count as first hdc)** and in each ch across: 14 hdc.
Rows 2-10: Ch 2 **(counts as first hdc)**, turn; hdc in next hdc and in each hdc across.
Finish off.

STITCH GUIDE

CLUSTER (uses one sp)
★ YO, insert hook in sp indicated, YO and pull up a loop, YO and draw through 2 loops on hook; repeat from ★ once **more**, YO and draw through all 3 loops on hook.

Vest is worked from side to side in one piece beginning at Left Front, then a lace edging is worked across each Front edge.

LEFT FRONT

With larger size hook, ch 122.

Row 1 (Right side)**:** Hdc in third ch from hook **(2 skipped chs count as first hdc)** and in each ch across: 121 hdc.

Note: Loop a short piece of yarn around any stitch to mark Row 1 as **right** side.

Row 2: Ch 2 **(counts as first hdc, now and throughout)**, turn; hdc in next hdc and in each hdc across.

Repeat Row 2 until Left Front measures approximately {12-12½}{13-13½-14}"/{30.5-32}{33-34.5-35.5} cm from beginning ch, ending by working a **wrong** side row.

LEFT ARMHOLE SHAPING

BODY

Row 1: Ch 2, turn; hdc in next {56-56}{53-53-50} hdc, leave remaining sts unworked: {57-57}{54-54-51} hdc.

Rows 2 and 3: Ch 2, turn; hdc in next hdc and in each hdc across.

Finish off.

NECK/SHOULDER EDGE

Row 1: With **right** side facing, skip next {32-32}{35-35-38} hdc from Body and join yarn with slip st in next hdc; ch 2, hdc in last 31 hdc: 32 hdc.

Rows 2 and 3: Ch 2, turn; hdc in next hdc and in each hdc across; do **not** finish off.

BACK

Row 1: Ch 2, turn; hdc in next hdc and in each hdc across; ch {32-32}{35-35-38}, being careful **not** to twist ch, hdc in each hdc across Row 3 of Body: 121 sts.

Row 2: Ch 2, turn; hdc in next hdc and in each hdc and each ch across.

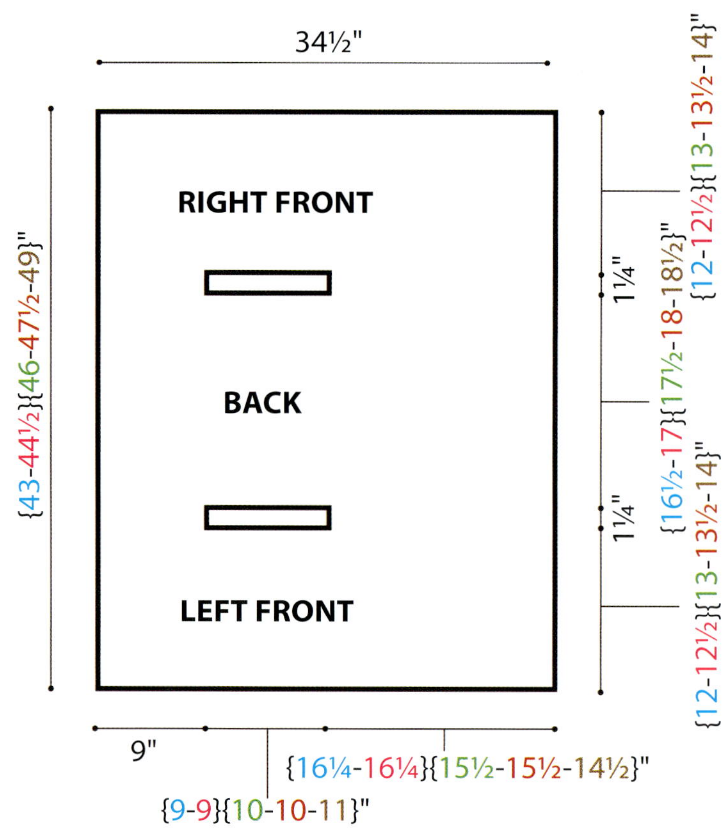

Row 3: Ch 2, turn; hdc in next hdc and in each hdc across.

Repeat Row 3 until Back measures approximately {16½-17}{17½-18-18½}"/{42-43}{44.5-45.5-47} cm from top of Armhole, ending by working a **wrong** side row.

RIGHT ARMHOLE SHAPING

Work same as Left Armhole Shaping.

RIGHT FRONT

Work same as Back until Right Front measures same as Left Front, ending by working a **wrong** side row.

RIGHT FRONT EDGING

Row 1: Ch 5 **(counts as first dc plus ch 2, now and throughout)**, turn; skip next hdc, ★ † sc in next hdc, ch 3, skip next 3 hdc, 5 dc in next hdc, ch 3, skip next 3 hdc, sc in next hdc †, ch 3, skip next hdc, dc in next hdc, ch 3, skip next hdc; repeat from ★ 8 times **more**, then repeat from † to † once, ch 2, skip next hdc, dc in last hdc: 10 5-dc groups and 40 sps.

Row 2: Ch 1, turn; sc in first dc, ★ ch 2, skip next 2 sps, dc in next dc, (ch 1, dc in next dc) 4 times, ch 2, skip next 2 sps, sc in next dc; repeat from ★ across: 10 5-dc groups and 60 sps.

Row 3: Ch 5, turn; ★ † skip next ch-2 sp, (work Cluster in next ch-1 sp, ch 2) 4 times, skip next ch-2 sp, dc in next sc †, ch 2; repeat from ★ 8 times **more**, then repeat from † to † once: 10 4-Cluster groups and 50 sps.

Row 4: Ch 5, turn; ★ † skip next ch-2 sp, (work Cluster in next ch-2 sp, ch 2) 3 times, skip next ch-2 sp, dc in next dc †, ch 2; repeat from ★ 8 times **more**, then repeat from † to † once: 10 3-Cluster groups and 40 sps.

Row 5: Ch 7 **(counts as first dc plus ch 4)**, turn; ★ † skip next ch-2 sp, work Cluster in next ch-2 sp, ch 2, work Cluster in next ch-2 sp, ch 4, skip next ch-2 sp, dc in next dc †, ch 4; repeat from ★ 8 times **more**, then repeat from † to † once: 10 2-Cluster groups and 30 sps.

Row 6: Ch 5, turn; ★ † dc in next ch-4 sp, ch 2, work Cluster in next ch-2 sp, ch 2, dc in next ch-4 sp, ch 2, dc in next dc †, ch 2; repeat from ★ 8 times **more**, then repeat from † to † once: 10 Clusters and 40 sps.

Row 7: Using smaller size hook, ch 1, turn; (sc, ch 3, 2 dc) in first dc, skip next ch-2 sp, ★ (sc, ch 3, 2 dc) in next st, skip next ch-2 sp; repeat from ★ across to last dc, sc in last dc; finish off.

LEFT FRONT EDGING

Row 1: With **right** side facing, using larger size hook, and working in free loops of beginning ch ***(Fig. 2, page 31)***, join yarn with slip st in first ch; ch 5, skip next ch, ★ † sc in next ch, ch 3, skip next 3 chs, 5 dc in next ch, ch 3, skip next 3 chs, sc in next ch †, ch 3, skip next ch, dc in next ch, ch 3, skip next ch; repeat from ★ 8 times **more**, then repeat from † to † once, ch 2, skip next ch, dc in next ch: 10 5-dc groups and 40 sps.

Rows 2-7: Work same as Right Front Edging; do **not** finish off.

Bottom Edging: Ch 1, sc evenly across end of rows along bottom edge; finish off.

Top Edging: With **right** side facing and working in end of rows along top edge, join yarn with slip st at corner; ch 1, sc evenly across; finish off.

hoodie

EASY

SHOPPING LIST

Yarn (Light Weight) LIGHT 3

[3.5 ounces, 326 yards

(100 grams, 299 meters) per skein]:

☐ {5-6}{6-7-8} skeins

Crochet Hooks

☐ Size G (4 mm)

or size needed for gauge

Additional Supplies

☐ Split ring marker

☐ Tapestry needle

☐ Sewing needle and thread

☐ 7/8" (22 mm) Buttons - 7

SIZE INFORMATION

Sizes	Finished Chest Measurement	
Large	42¼"	(107 cm)
1X	46"	(117 cm)
2X	50"	(127 cm)
3X	53¾"	(136.5 cm)
4X	58¼"	(148 cm)

Size Note: We have printed the instructions for the sizes in different colors to make it easier for you to find:

- Size Large in Blue
- Size 1X in Pink
- Size 2X in Green
- Size 3X in Orange
- Size 4X in Brown

Instructions in Black apply to all sizes.

GAUGE INFORMATION

17 hdc and 11 rows = 4" (10 cm)

Gauge Swatch: 4" (10 cm) square

Ch 18.

Row 1: Hdc in third ch from hook **(2 skipped chs count as first hdc)** and in each ch across: 17 hdc.

Rows 2-11: Ch 2 **(counts as first hdc)**, turn; hdc in next hdc and in each hdc across.

Finish off.

STITCH GUIDE

HALF DOUBLE CROCHET 2 TOGETHER ***(abbreviated hdc2tog)***

(uses next 2 sts)

(YO, insert hook in **next** st, YO and pull up a loop) twice, YO and draw through all 5 loops on hook **(counts as one hdc)**.

BACK

BODY

Ch {91-99}{107-115-125}.

Row 1 (Right side)**:** Hdc in third ch from hook **(2 skipped chs count as first hdc, now and throughout)** and in each ch across: {90-98}{106-114-124} hdc.

Note: Loop a short piece of yarn around any stitch to mark Row 1 as **right** side.

Row 2: Ch 2 **(counts as first hdc, now and throughout)**, turn; hdc in next hdc and in each hdc across.

Repeat Row 2 until Back measures approximately 17" (43 cm) from beginning ch, ending by working a **wrong** side row.

ARMHOLE SHAPING

Row 1: Turn; slip st in first {5-6}{7-8-9} hdc, ch 2, hdc in next hdc and in each hdc across to last {4-5}{6-7-8} hdc, leave remaining sts unworked: {82-88}{94-100-108} hdc.

Row 2: Turn; slip st in first {3-4}{5-6-7} hdc, ch 2, hdc in next hdc and in each hdc across to last {2-3}{4-5-6} hdc, leave remaining hdc unworked: {78-82}{86-90-96} hdc.

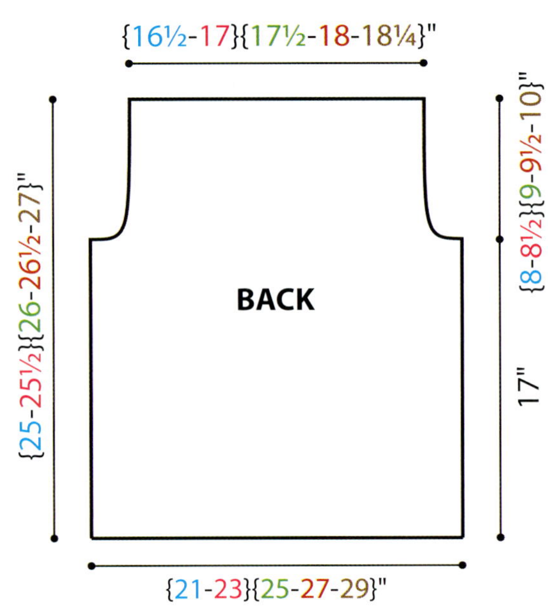

Row 3 (Decrease row)**:** Ch 2, turn; hdc2tog, hdc in each hdc across to last 3 hdc, hdc2tog, hdc in last hdc: {76-80}{84-88-94} hdc.

Repeat Row 3, {1-2}{3-6-8} time(s): {74-76}{78-76-78} hdc.

SIZES LARGE, 1X, & 2X ONLY

Continue to decrease one stitch at **each** edge in same manner, every other row twice: {70-72}{74} hdc.

ALL SIZES

Work even until Back measures approximately {25-25½}{26-26½-27}"/{63.5-65}{66-67.5-68.5} cm from beginning ch, ending by working a **wrong** side row; finish off.

POCKET LINING (Make 2)

Ch 31.

Work same as Back until Pocket Lining measures approximately 4½" (11.5 cm) from beginning ch, ending by working a **wrong** side row; finish off leaving a long end for sewing: 30 hdc.

LEFT FRONT

BODY

Ch {51-55}{59-63-68}.

Row 1 (Right side)**:** Hdc in third ch from hook and in each ch across: {50-54}{58-62-67} hdc.

Note: Mark Row 1 as **right** side.

Row 2: Ch 2, turn; hdc in next hdc and in each hdc across.

Repeat Row 2 until Left Front measures approximately 5" (12.5 cm) from beginning ch, ending by working a **wrong** side row.

Pocket Placement Row: Ch 2, turn; hdc in next {9-11}{13-15-17} hdc, holding Pocket Lining **behind** work with **right** side facing, hdc in each hdc across, skip next 30 hdc on Left Front, hdc in next hdc and in each hdc across.

Repeat Row 2 until Left Front measures same as Back to Armhole Shaping, ending by working a **wrong** side row.

ARMHOLE SHAPING

Row 1: Turn; slip st in first {5-6}{7-8-9} hdc, ch 2, hdc in next hdc and in each hdc across: {46-49}{52-55-59} hdc.

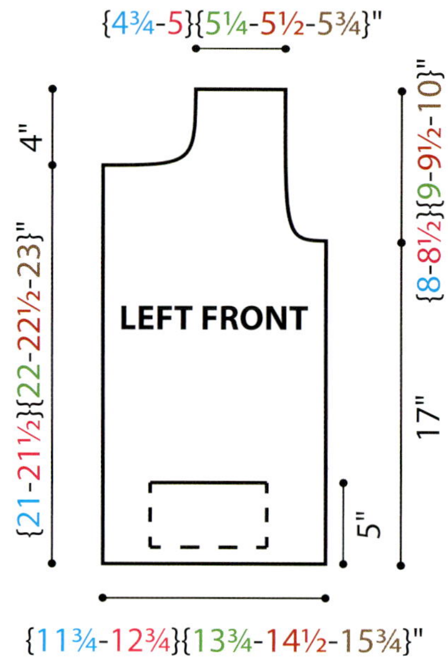

Row 2: Ch 2, turn; hdc in next hdc and in each hdc across to last {2-3}{4-5-6} hdc, leave remaining hdc unworked: {44-46}{48-50-53} hdc.

Row 3 (Decrease row)**:** Ch 2, turn; hdc2tog, hdc in each hdc across: {43-45}{47-49-52} hdc.

Row 4 (Decrease row)**:** Ch 2, turn; hdc in next hdc and in each hdc across to last 3 hdc, hdc2tog, hdc in last hdc: {42-44}{46-48-51} hdc.

Continue to decrease one stitch at Armhole edge in same manner, every row, {0-1}{2-5-7} time(s) ***(see Zeros, page 30)***; then decrease every other row, {2-2}{2-0-0} times: {40-41}{42-43-44} hdc.

Work even until Left Front measures approximately {21-21½}{22-22½-23}"/{53.5-54.5}{56-57-58.5} cm from beginning ch, ending by working a **right** side row.

NECK SHAPING

Row 1: Turn; slip st in first 12 hdc, ch 2, hdc in next hdc and in each hdc across: {29-30}{31-32-33} hdc.

Row 2: Ch 2, turn; hdc in next hdc and in each hdc across to last 3 hdc, leave remaining hdc unworked: {26-27}{28-29-30} hdc.

Row 3: Turn; slip st in first 3 hdc, ch 2, hdc in next hdc and in each hdc across: {24-25}{26-27-28} hdc.

Decrease one stitch at Neck edge, every row, 3 times; then decrease every other row once: {20-21}{22-23-24} hdc.

Work even until Left Front measures same as Back, ending by working a **wrong** side row; finish off leaving a long end for sewing.

Place markers for 7 buttons, placing one on Row 4, one on the fifth row before the Neck Shaping, and 5 evenly spaced between both markers.

RIGHT FRONT

BODY

Work same as Left Front through Row 3.

Buttonhole Row: Ch 2, turn; hdc in next hdc and in each hdc across to last 6 hdc, ch 2, skip next 2 hdc **(buttonhole made)**, hdc in last 4 hdc: {48-52}{56-60-65} hdc and one ch-2 sp.

Work 6 more buttonholes when Right Front measures same as markers on Left Front.

Continue to work same as Left Front including working across Pocket Lining to Armhole Shaping, ending by working a **wrong** side row.

ARMHOLE SHAPING

Row 1: Ch 2, turn; hdc in next hdc and in each hdc across to last {4-5}{6-7-8} hdc, leave remaining hdc unworked: {46-49}{52-55-59} hdc.

Row 2: Turn; slip st in first {3-4}{5-6-7} hdc, ch 2, hdc in next hdc and in each hdc across: {44-46}{48-50-53} hdc.

Row 3 (Decrease row)**:** Ch 2, turn; hdc in next hdc and in each hdc across to last 3 hdc, hdc2tog, hdc in last hdc: {43-45}{47-49-52} hdc.

Row 4 (Decrease row)**:** Ch 2, turn; hdc2tog, hdc in each hdc across: {42-44}{46-48-51} hdc.

Continue to decrease one stitch at Armhole edge in same manner, every row, {0-1}{2-5-7} time(s); then decrease every other row, {2-2}{2-0-0} times: {40-41}{42-43-44} hdc.

Work even until Right Front measures same as Left Front, ending by working a **right** side row.

NECK SHAPING

Row 1: Ch 2, turn; hdc in next hdc and in each hdc across to last 11 hdc, leave remaining hdc unworked: {29-30}{31-32-33} hdc.

Row 2: Turn; slip st in first 4 hdc, ch 2, hdc in next hdc and in each hdc across: {26-27}{28-29-30} hdc.

Row 3: Ch 2, turn; hdc in next hdc and in each hdc across to last 2 hdc, leave remaining hdc unworked: {24-25}{26-27-28} hdc.

Decrease one stitch at Neck edge, every row, 3 times; then decrease every other row once: {20-21}{22-23-24} hdc.

Work even until Right Front measures same as Left Front, ending by working a **wrong** side row; finish off leaving a long end for sewing.

SLEEVE (Make 2)

BODY

Ch {41-43}{43-43-43}.

Row 1 (Right side)**:** Hdc in third ch from hook and in each ch across: {40-42}{42-42-42} hdc.

Note: Mark Row 1 as **right** side.

Row 2: Ch 2, turn; hdc in next hdc and in each hdc across.

Row 3 (Increase row)**:** Ch 2, turn; hdc in first hdc and in each hdc across to last hdc, 2 hdc in last hdc: {42-44}{44-44-44} hdc.

Continue to increase one stitch at **each** edge in same manner, every other row, {0-0}{3-9-15} times; then increase every fourth row, {5-11}{10-7-4} times; then increase every sixth row, {4-0}{0-0-0} times: {60-66}{70-76-82} hdc.

Work even until Body measures approximately 18½" (47 cm) from beginning ch, ending by working a **wrong** side row.

SLEEVE CAP

Row 1: Turn; slip st in first {5-6}{7-8-9} hdc, ch 2, hdc in next hdc and in each hdc across to last {4-5}{6-7-8} hdc, leave remaining hdc unworked: {52-56}{58-62-66} hdc.

Row 2 (Decrease row)**:** Ch 2, turn; hdc2tog twice, hdc across to last 5 hdc, hdc2tog twice, hdc in last hdc: {48-52}{54-58-62} hdc.

Repeat Row 2, {1-2}{2-2-3} time(s): {44-44}{46-50-50} hdc.

Decrease **one** stitch at **each** edge, every row, {11-11}{12-14-14} times: 22 hdc.

Last 2 Rows: Turn; slip st in first 3 sts, ch 2, hdc in next hdc and in each hdc across to last 2 sts, leave remaining sts unworked: 14 hdc.

Finish off.

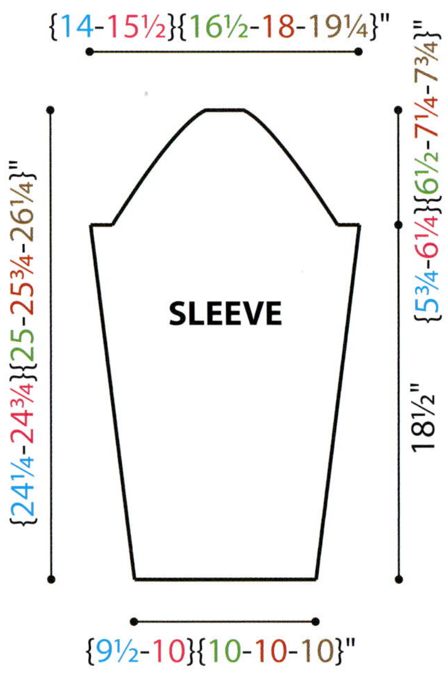

FINISHING

POCKET EDGING

Row 1: With **right** side of either Front facing, join yarn with slip st in first skipped hdc on Pocket Placement Row; ch 1, sc in same st and in each hdc across: 30 sc.

Row 2: Ch 1, turn; sc in each sc across; finish off.

Repeat on second Front.

Sew Edging and Pocket Linings in place.

Whipstitch Front to Back at shoulders *(Fig. 3a, page 31)*.

HOOD

Row 1: With **right** side facing, join yarn with slip st in first unworked hdc on Right Front Neck Shaping; ch 2, work 25 hdc evenly spaced across Right Front neck edge, hdc in each hdc across Back, work 26 hdc evenly spaced across Left Front neck edge: 82 hdc.

Rows 2 and 3: Ch 2, turn; hdc in next hdc and in each hdc across.

Row 4: Ch 2, turn; hdc in next 41 hdc, place marker around each of last 2 hdc made for increase placement (center 2 hdc), hdc in last 40 hdc.

Row 5 (Increase row)**:** Ch 2, turn; hdc in next hdc and in each hdc across working 2 hdc in both marked hdc and moving markers to first and last hdc of the increased sts: 84 hdc.

Continue to work 2 hdc in each marked hdc every fifth row, 4 times, moving markers in same manner: 92 hdc.

Work even until Hood measures approximately 12½" (32 cm), ending by working a **wrong** side row; finish off leaving a long end for sewing.

Fold last row in half with **wrong** side together and whipstitch top seam.

Sew Sleeves to Armholes, matching center of last row on Sleeve Cap to shoulder seam.

Whipstitch underarm and side in one continuous seam *(Fig. 3b, page 31)*.

Sew buttons to Left Front at markers.

a-line top

EASY

SHOPPING LIST

Yarn (Medium Weight) 4

[3.5 ounces, 186 yards
(100 grams, 170 meters) per skein]:

- ☐ {7-8}{9-10-10} skeins

Crochet Hooks

- ☐ Size G (4 mm)
- ☐ Size H (5 mm)

or sizes needed for gauge

Additional Supplies

- ☐ Yarn needle

SIZE INFORMATION

Sizes	Finished Chest Measurement	
Large	41½"	(105.5 cm)
1X	47"	(119.5 cm)
2X	51¾"	(131.5 cm)
3X	57½"	(146 cm)
4X	62"	(157.5 cm)

Size Note: We have printed the instructions for the sizes in different colors to make it easier for you to find:

- Size Large in Blue
- Size 1X in Pink
- Size 2X in Green
- Size 3X in Orange
- Size 4X in Brown

Instructions in Black apply to all sizes.

GAUGE INFORMATION

With smaller size hook,

17 hdc and 13 rows = 4" (10 cm)

Gauge Swatch: 4" (10 cm) square

With smaller size hook, ch 18.

Row 1: Hdc in third ch from hook **(2 skipped chs count as first hdc)** and in each ch across: 17 hdc.

Rows 2-13: Ch 2 **(counts as first hdc)**, turn; hdc in next hdc and in each hdc across.

Finish off.

STITCH GUIDE

SINGLE CROCHET 2 TOGETHER ***(abbreviated sc2tog)***

Pull up a loop in each of next 2 sts, YO and draw through all 3 loops on hook **(counts as one sc)**.

SINGLE CROCHET 3 TOGETHER ***(abbreviated sc3tog)***

Pull up a loop in each of next 3 sts, YO and draw through all 4 loops on hook **(counts as one sc)**.

HALF DOUBLE CROCHET 2 TOGETHER ***(abbreviated hdc2tog)*** (uses next 2 sts)

(YO, insert hook in **next** st, YO and pull up a loop) twice, YO and draw through all 5 loops on hook **(counts as one hdc)**.

BACK

LACE PATTERN

With larger size hook, ch {135-151} {167-183-199}.

Row 1 (Right side)**:** Sc in second ch from hook and in next 5 chs, ★ ch 2, skip next 4 chs, 3 dc in each of next 2 chs, ch 2, skip next 4 chs, sc in next 6 chs; repeat from ★ across: {8-9}{10-11-12} 6-dc groups and {9-10}{11-12-13} 6-sc groups.

Note: Loop a short piece of yarn around any stitch to mark Row 1 as **right** side.

Row 2: Ch 3 **(counts as first dc, now and throughout)**, turn; dc in next 5 sc, ★ ch 4, skip next 2 dc, sc in next 2 dc, ch 4, skip next 2 dc, dc in next 6 sc; repeat from ★ across: {9-10} {11-12-13} 6-dc groups and {16-18} {20-22-24} sc.

Row 3: Ch 1, turn; sc in first 6 dc, ★ ch 2, 3 dc in each of next 2 sc, ch 2, sc in next 6 dc; repeat from ★ across: {8-9}{10-11-12} 6-dc groups and {9-10}{11-12-13} 6-sc groups.

Rows 4-12: Repeat Rows 2 and 3, 4 times; then repeat Row 2 once **more**.

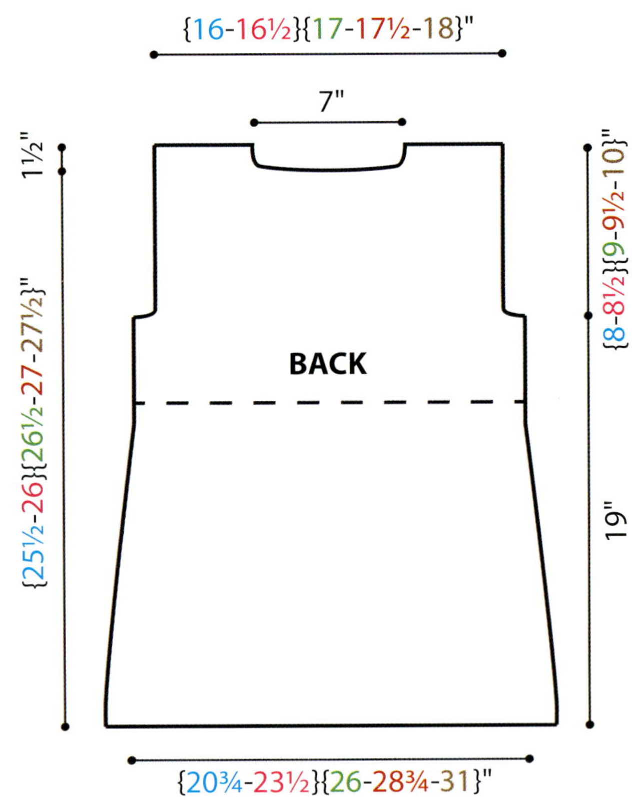

Row 13 (Decrease row)**:** Ch 1, turn; sc in first 2 dc, sc2tog, sc in next 2 dc, ★ ch 2, 3 dc in each of next 2 sc, ch 2, sc in next 2 dc, sc2tog, sc in next 2 dc; repeat from ★ across: {8-9}{10-11-12} 6-dc groups and {9-10}{11-12-13} 5-sc groups.

Row 14: Ch 3, turn; dc in next 4 sc, ★ ch 4, skip next 2 dc, sc in next 2 dc, ch 4, skip next 2 dc, dc in next 5 sc; repeat from ★ across: {9-10}{11-12-13} 5-dc groups and {16-18}{20-22-24} sc.

Row 15: Ch 1, turn; sc in first 5 dc, ★ ch 2, 3 dc in each of next 2 sc, ch 2, sc in next 5 dc; repeat from ★ across: {8-9}{10-11-12} 6-dc groups and {9-10}{11-12-13} 5-sc groups.

Rows 16-24: Repeat Rows 14 and 15, 4 times; then repeat Row 14 once **more**.

Row 25 (Decrease row)**:** Ch 1, turn; beginning in first dc, sc2tog, sc in next dc, sc2tog, ★ ch 2, 3 dc in each of next 2 sc, ch 2, skip next ch-4 sp, sc2tog, sc in next dc, sc2tog; repeat from ★ across: {8-9}{10-11-12} 6-dc groups and {9-10}{11-12-13} 3-sc groups.

Row 26: Ch 3, turn; dc in next 2 sc, ★ ch 4, skip next 2 dc, sc in next 2 dc, ch 4, skip next 2 dc, dc in next 3 sc; repeat from ★ across: {9-10}{11-12-13} 3-dc groups and {16-18}{20-22-24} sc.

Row 27: Ch 1, turn; sc in first 3 dc, ★ ch 2, 3 dc in each of next 2 sc, ch 2, sc in next 3 dc; repeat from ★ across: {8-9}{10-11-12} 6-dc groups and {9-10}{11-12-13} 3-sc groups.

Rows 28-36: Repeat Rows 26 and 27, 4 times; then repeat Row 26 once **more**.

Row 37 (Decrease row)**:** Ch 1, turn; beginning in first dc, sc3tog, ★ ch 2, 3 dc in each of next 2 sc, ch 2, skip next ch-4 sp, sc3tog; repeat from ★ across: {8-9}{10-11-12} 6-dc groups and {9-10}{11-12-13} sc.

Row 38: Ch 7 **(counts as first dc plus ch 4)**, turn; skip next 2 dc, sc in next 2 dc, ch 4, skip next 2 dc, dc in next sc, ★ ch 4, skip next 2 dc, sc in next 2 dc, ch 4, skip next 2 dc, dc in next sc; repeat from ★ across: {9-10}{11-12-13} dc and {16-18}{20-22-24} sc.

Row 39: Ch 1, turn; sc in first dc, ★ ch 2, 3 dc in each of next 2 sc, ch 2, sc in next dc; repeat from ★ across: {8-9}{10-11-12} 6-dc groups and {9-10}{11-12-13} sc.

Rows 40-48: Repeat Rows 38 and 39, 4 times, then repeat Row 38 once **more**.

BODY

Change to smaller size hook.

Row 1: Ch 2 **(counts as first hdc, now and throughout)**, turn; {3-4}{3-4-3} hdc in next ch-4 sp, hdc in next 2 sc, 4 hdc in next ch-4 sp, hdc in next dc, ★ 4 hdc in next ch-4 sp, hdc in next 2 sc, 4 hdc in next ch-4 sp, hdc in next dc; repeat from ★ across: {88-100}{110-122-132} hdc.

Row 2: Ch 2, turn; hdc in next hdc and in each hdc across.

Repeat Row 2 until Back measures approximately 19" (48.5 cm) from beginning ch, ending by working a **wrong** side row.

ARMHOLE SHAPING

Row 1: Turn; slip st in first {5-7}{9-11-13} hdc, ch 2, hdc in next hdc and in each hdc across to last {4-6}{8-10-12} hdc, leave remaining hdc unworked: {80-88}{94-102-108} hdc.

Row 2: Turn; slip st in first {3-4}{6-7-8} hdc, ch 2, hdc in next hdc and in each hdc across to last {2-3}{5-6-7} hdc, leave remaining hdc unworked: {76-82}{84-90-94} hdc.

Row 3 (Decrease row)**:** Ch 2, turn; hdc2tog, hdc in each hdc across to last 3 hdc, hdc2tog, hdc in last hdc: {74-80}{82-88-92} hdc.

Repeat Row 3, {3-5}{5-7-8} times: {68-70}{72-74-76} hdc.

Work even until Back measures approximately {25½-26}{26½-27-27½}"/{65-66}{67.5-68.5-70} cm from beginning ch, ending by working a **wrong** side row.

RIGHT NECK SHAPING

Row 1: Ch 2, turn; hdc in next {19-20}{21-22-23} hdc, leave remaining hdc unworked: {20-21}{22-23-24} hdc.

Row 2: Ch 2, turn; hdc2tog, hdc in each hdc across: {19-20}{21-22-23} hdc.

Rows 3-5: Ch 2, turn; hdc in next hdc and in each hdc across.

Finish off.

LEFT NECK SHAPING

Row 1: With **right** side facing, skip 28 hdc from Right Neck Shaping and join yarn with slip st in next hdc; ch 2, hdc in next hdc and in each hdc across: {20-21}{22-23-24} hdc.

Row 2: Ch 2, turn; hdc in next hdc and in each hdc across to last 3 hdc, hdc2tog, hdc in last hdc: {19-20}{21-22-23} hdc.

Rows 3-5: Ch 2, turn; hdc in next hdc and in each hdc across.

Finish off.

FRONT

Work same as Back through Row {2-4}{4-6-8} of Armhole Shaping: {76-78}{80-82-82} hdc.

LEFT NECK SHAPING

Row 1: Ch 2, turn; hdc2tog, hdc in next {35-36}{37-38-38} hdc, leave remaining hdc unworked: {37-38}{39-40-40} hdc.

Row 2: Ch 2, turn; hdc2tog, hdc in each hdc across to last 3 hdc, hdc2tog, hdc in last hdc: {35-36}{37-38-38} hdc.

Repeat Row 2, {2-2}{2-2-1} time(s): {31-32}{33-34-36} hdc.

Continue to decrease one stitch at Neck edge in same manner, every row, {5-5}{5-5-6} times; then decrease every other row, 7 times: {19-20}{21-22-23} hdc.

Work even if needed for Armhole to measure same as Back, ending by working a **wrong** side row; finish off leaving a long end for sewing.

RIGHT NECK SHAPING

Row 1: With **right** side facing, join yarn with slip st in next unworked hdc on Front; ch 2, hdc in next hdc and in each hdc across to last 3 hdc, hdc2tog, hdc in last hdc: {37-38}{39-40-40} hdc.

Complete same as Left Neck Shaping.

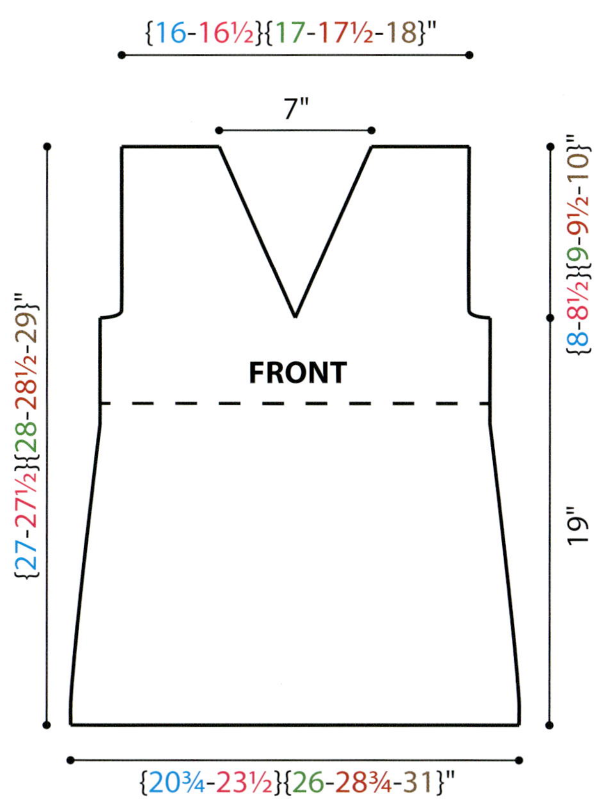

FINISHING

LOWER BACK EDGING

Row 1: With **right** side facing, using larger size hook, and working in free loops of beginning ch *(Fig. 2, page 31)*, join yarn with slip st in first ch; ch 1, sc in same st and in next 5 chs, ★ 3 sc in next ch-4 sp, (dc, ch 1, dc) in next ch, ch 3, slip st in third ch from hook, (dc, ch 1, dc) in next ch, 3 sc in next ch-4 sp, sc in next 6 chs; repeat from ★ across; finish off.

LOWER FRONT EDGING

Work same as Lower Back Edging.

Whipstitch Front to Back at shoulders *(Fig. 3a, page 31)*.

Whipstitch side seam *(Fig. 3b, page 31)*.

NECK EDGING

Rnd 1: With **right** side facing and using smaller size hook, join yarn with slip st at left shoulder seam; ch 1, sc evenly around working sc2tog at center of Front; join with slip st to first sc.

Rnd 2: Ch 1, do **not** turn; working from **left** to **right**, work reverse sc in each sc around *(Figs. 4a-d, page 31)*; join with slip st to first st, finish off.

ARMHOLE EDGING

Rnd 1: With **right** side facing and using smaller size hook, join yarn with slip st at side seam; ch 1, sc evenly around; join with slip st to first sc.

Rnd 2: Ch 1, do **not** turn; working from **left** to **right**, work reverse sc in each sc around; join with slip st to first st, finish off.

Repeat for second Armhole.

general instructions

ABBREVIATIONS

BPdc	Back Post double crochet(s)
ch(s)	chain(s)
cm	centimeters
dc	double crochet(s)
FPdc	Front Post double crochet(s)
FPdtr	Front Post double treble crochet(s)
FPtr	Front Post treble crochet(s)
hdc	half double crochet(s)
hdc2tog	half double crochet 2 together
mm	millimeters
Rnd(s)	Round(s)
sc	single crochet(s)
sc2tog	single crochet 2 together
sc3tog	single crochet 3 together
sp(s)	space(s)
st(s)	stitch(es)
YO	yarn over

SYMBOLS & TERMS

★ — work instructions following ★ as many **more** times as indicated in addition to the first time.

† to † — work all instructions from first † to second † **as many** times as specified.

( ) or **[ ]** — work enclosed instructions **as many** times as specified by the number immediately following **or** work all enclosed instructions in the stitch or space indicated **or** contains explanatory remarks.

colon (:) — the number(s) given after a colon at the end of a row or round denote(s) the number of stitches or spaces you should have on that row or round.

work even — work without increasing or decreasing in the established pattern.

GAUGE

Exact gauge is **essential** for proper fit. Before beginning your project, make the sample swatch given in the individual instructions in the yarn and hook specified. After completing the swatch, measure it, counting your stitches and rows carefully. If your swatch is larger or smaller than specified, **make another, changing hook size to get the correct gauge.** Keep trying until you find the size hook that will give you the specified gauge. Once proper gauge is obtained, measure width of piece approximately every 3" (7.5 cm) to be sure gauge remains consistent.

ZEROS

To consolidate the length of an involved pattern, zeros are sometimes used so that all sizes can be combined. For example, repeat Row 3, {0-0}{5-8-9} times means the first 2 sizes would do nothing and the remaining sizes would work as indicated.

Yarn Weight Symbol & Names	LACE 0	SUPER FINE 1	FINE 2	LIGHT 3	MEDIUM 4	BULKY 5	SUPER BULKY 6	JUMBO 7
Type of Yarns in Category	Fingering, size 10 crochet thread	Sock, Fingering, Baby	Sport, Baby	DK, Light Worsted	Worsted, Afghan, Aran	Chunky, Craft, Rug	Super Bulky, Roving	Jumbo, Roving
Crochet Gauge* Ranges in Single Crochet to 4" (10 cm)	32-42 sts**	21-32 sts	16-20 sts	12-17 sts	11-14 sts	8-11 sts	6-9 sts	5 sts and fewer
Advised Hook Size Range	Steel*** 6 to 8, Regular hook B-1	B-1 to E-4	E-4 to 7	7 to I-9	I-9 to K-10½	K-10½ to M/N-13	M/N-13 to Q	Q and larger

*GUIDELINES ONLY: The chart above reflects the most commonly used gauges and hook sizes for specific yarn categories.

** Lace weight yarns are usually crocheted with larger hooks to create lacy openwork patterns. Accordingly, a gauge range is difficult to determine. Always follow the gauge stated in your pattern.

*** Steel crochet hooks are sized differently from regular hooks–the higher the number, the smaller the hook, which is the reverse of regular hook sizing.

CROCHET TERMINOLOGY		
UNITED STATES		INTERNATIONAL
slip stitch (slip st)	=	single crochet (sc)
single crochet (sc)	=	double crochet (dc)
half double crochet (hdc)	=	half treble crochet (htr)
double crochet (dc)	=	treble crochet (tr)
treble crochet (tr)	=	double treble crochet (dtr)
double treble crochet (dtr)	=	triple treble crochet (ttr)
triple treble crochet (tr tr)	=	quadruple treble crochet (qtr)
skip	=	miss

POST STITCH

Work around post of stitch indicated, inserting hook in direction of arrow ***(Fig. 1)***.

Fig. 1

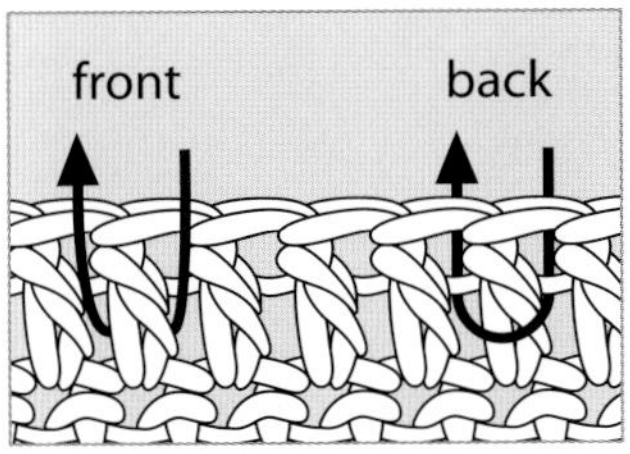

FREE LOOPS OF A CHAIN

When instructed to work in free loops of a chain, work in loop indicated by arrow ***(Fig. 2)***.

Fig. 2

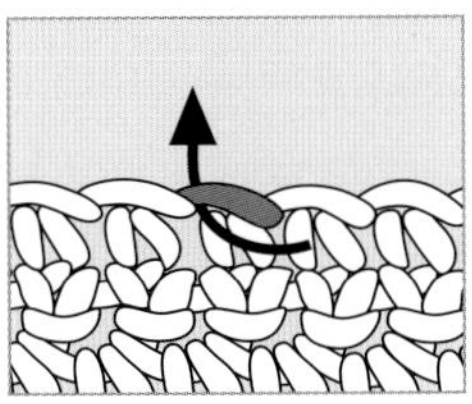

BEGINNER	Projects for first-time crocheters using basic stitches. Minimal shaping.
EASY	Projects using yarn with basic stitches, repetitive stitch patterns, simple color changes, and simple shaping and finishing.
INTERMEDIATE	Projects using a variety of techniques, such as basic lace patterns or color patterns, mid-level shaping and finishing.
EXPERIENCED	Projects with intricate stitch patterns, techniques and dimension, such as non-repeating patterns, multi-color techniques, fine threads, small hooks, detailed shaping and refined finishing.

WHIPSTITCH

With **wrong** sides together, sew through both pieces once to secure the beginning of the seam, leaving an ample yarn end to weave in later. Insert the needle from **right** to **left** through two strands on each stitch of each piece ***(Fig. 3a)*** **or** through ends of rows ***(Fig. 3b)***. Bring the needle around and insert it from **right** to **left** through the next strands on both pieces.

Repeat along the edge, being careful to match stitches and rows.

Fig. 3a

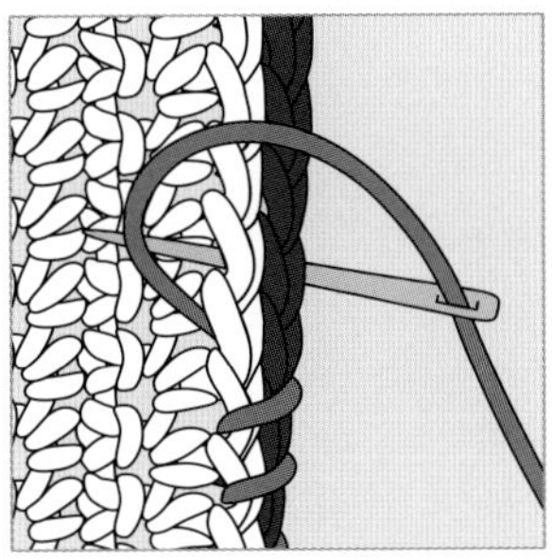

Fig. 3b

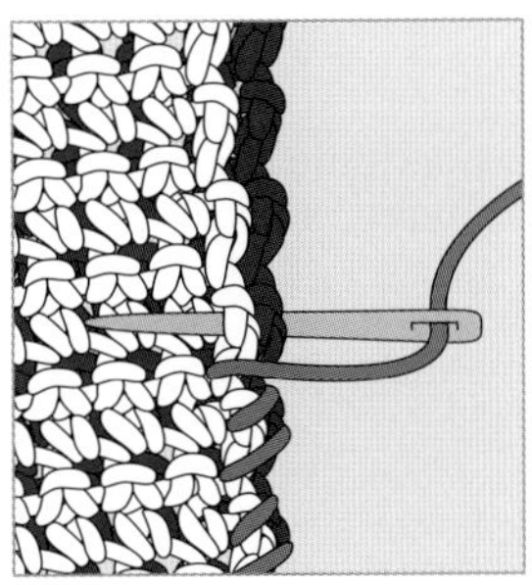

REVERSE SINGLE CROCHET

(abbreviated reverse sc)

Working from **left** to **right**, insert hook in stitch to right of hook ***(Fig. 4a)***, YO and draw through, under and to left of loop on hook (2 loops on hook) ***(Fig. 4b)***, YO and draw through both loops on hook ***(Fig. 4c)*** **(reverse sc made, *Fig. 4d*)**.

Fig. 4a

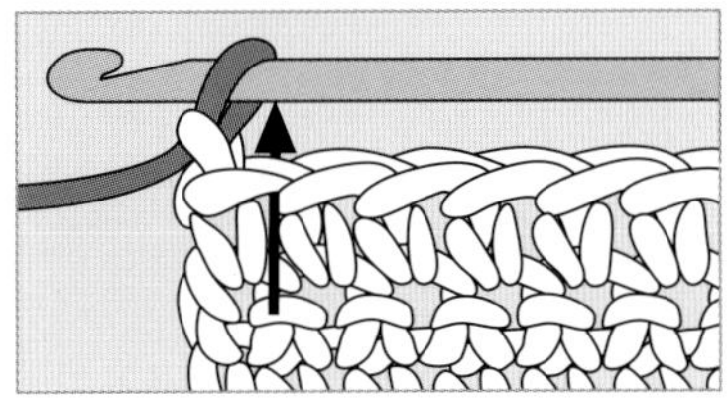

Fig. 4b

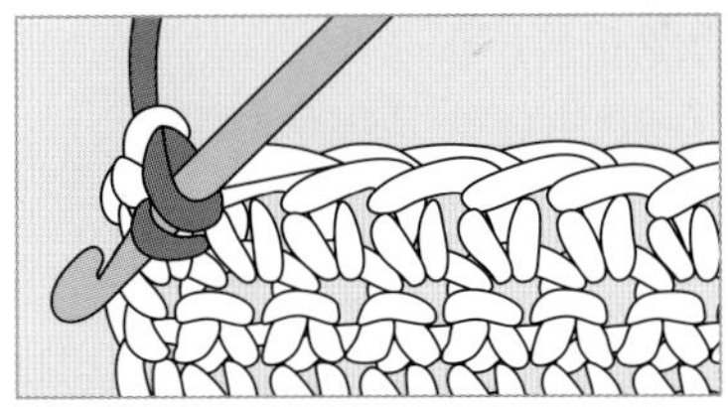

Fig. 4c

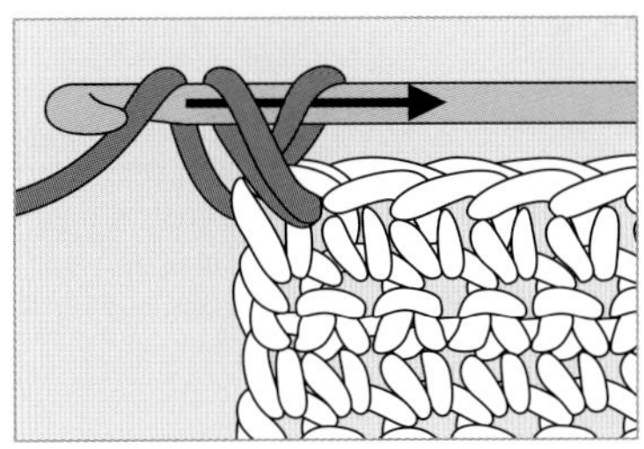

Fig. 4d

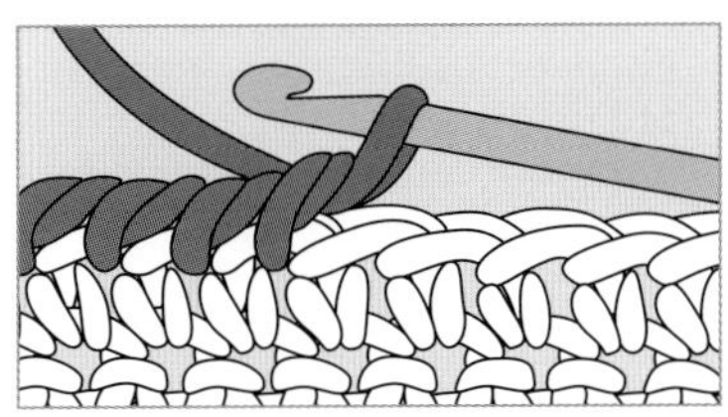

CROCHET HOOKS																	
U.S.	B-1	C-2	D-3	E-4	F-5	G-6	7	H-8	I-9	J-10	K-10½	L-11	M/N-13	N/P-15	P/Q	Q	S
Metric - mm	2.25	2.75	3.25	3.5	3.75	4	4.5	5	5.5	6	6.5	8	9	10	15	16	19

yarn information

The garments in this book were made using a variety of yarns. Any brand of the specific weight of yarn may be used. It is best to refer to the yardage/meters when determining how many balls or skeins to purchase. Remember, to arrive at the finished size, it is the GAUGE/TENSION that is important, not the brand of yarn.

For your convenience, listed below are the yarns used to create our photography models. Because yarn manufacturers make frequent changes in their product lines, you may sometimes find it necessary to use a substitute yarn or to search for the discontinued product at alternate suppliers (locally or online).

TUNIC
Red Heart® Unforgettable®
#3944 Bistro

UNCONSTRUCTED JACKET
Lion Brand® Sock-Ease™
#178 Snow Cone

BOXY CARDI
Lion Brand® Textures®
#200 Sun Rays

DRAPEY VEST
Lion Brand® Vanna's Style
#174 Olive

HOODIE
Red Heart® Cutie Pie™
#419 Koala

A-LINE TOP
Lion Brand® 24/7 Cotton®
#110 Navy

We have made every effort to ensure that these instructions are accurate and complete. We cannot, however, be responsible for human error, typographical mistakes, or variations in individual work.

Items made and instructions tested by Raymelle Greening, Amanda Loggins, and Stacey Williams.

Production Team: Instructional/Technical Editor - Cathy Hardy; Editorial Writer - Susan Frantz Wiles; Graphic Artist - Victoria Temple; Senior Graphic Artist - Lora Puls; Photo Stylist - Lori Wenger; and Photographer - Jason Masters.

Meet the Designer
Melissa Leapman

With more than 800 knit and crochet designs in print, Melissa Leapman is one of the most widely published designers working today.

She began her design career by freelancing for leading ready-to-wear design houses in New York City. She also created designs to help top yarn companies promote their new and existing yarns each season. Her ability to quickly develop fully envisioned garments put her skills in great demand.

Through the years, Leisure Arts has published more than 40 books of Melissa's fabulous designs. Melissa is also the host of several Leisure Arts DVDs in the best-selling teach-yourself series, "I Can't Believe I'm Knitting" and "I Can't Believe I'm Crocheting."

Nationally, her designs have been featured in numerous magazines, and her workshops on knitting and crochet are consistently popular with crafters of all skill levels. She has taught at major events such as STITCHES, Vogue Knitting LIVE, and The Knitting Guild Association conferences, as well as at hundreds of yarn shops and local guild events across the country.

To find more of Melissa's designs, visit LeisureArts.com, Melissa's Facebook page, and Ravelry.com.